NOT FOR YOUR CONVENIENCE

Audrey Sapunarich

D1403111

Dad, Maria, Heather, Megan, Karlee, Josh, Kayleigh, and Jes,

I will cherish your influence and support for the rest of my life.

Love is so short, forgetting is so long.

– Neruda

<u>1</u>

What Is Left

a dusty cookbook
and a daughter –
this is what he has left of the love of his life.

when he goes to the cabinet
in the house he built for her
and hands you a card
out of that cookbook,
says *I been craving this,*

go to the store,
get the ingredients,
and make it.

make it no matter how tired you are,
how much snow is outside,
how many other things
you have to do.

make it because this is what he has left of the love of his life –
a dusty cookbook
and a daughter.

Excerpts of a Kitchen Notebook

I was raised by a man of few words,
a man who often misspelled those words
but saved me over and over again
with those words.
A man who worked all day
and came home every night
covered in grease
to teach his daughter.
Spell "because," he said
looking at the book, following each letter
and applauding me,
teaching me how to write and read
words he himself couldn't spell.

When I got older and my mother left,
I tried to teach myself how to cook.
The note read,
flowr, egg, milk
That's how you bread the chicken.
Dont let the bull shit get to you,
This aint your fault Audrey
I love you so much what else can I say
That's how you heal a wound.
Be happy
Do what ever you want to do
Go to what ever school you want
Dont worry about the money
That's how you sacrifice for your kid.

I was raised by a man of few words,
a man who often misspelled those words
but saved me over and over again
with those words.

He crumbles up papers, throwing them in the trash.
Audrey, will you write this letter for me?
It's important and your handwriting is better.
You spell everything right, he says.
My hand effortlessly, properly
jots the words just as he taught me to as a child.

You're a great writer, he always says.
It's funny because
I was raised by man of few words,
a man who often misspelled those words
and he is
the greatest writer I know.

Giving Up The Gold

When dad was young,
he had money for tricked out cars
and on the weekends,
he had bar fights after too many screwdrivers.
He had leather jackets, gold chains, long hair,
and bloodshot eyes behind big sunglasses.
He had Woodstock '94
and his buddy puking on the windshield
jamming to Foghat.
He went to bed when everybody else was getting up
and he never wanted a kid.

Now dad has faded t-shirts and bandanas
and on the weekends, he splits wood
and watches hummingbirds with his morning coffee.
All those jeans from when he was 25 still fit
and he gets up at 4:30 a.m. to go to work
in a rusted four-door
with a vanilla air freshener.
After work, he has a beer
and falls asleep on the couch by 10.
He's got a kid, '93
that he works his ass off to put through college,
a kid who plays Bachman-Turner Overdrive
when they're cooking dinner
and gets him going about the good old days,
who finds his gold bracelet stuffed in a hidden box
and puts it on
with no intention of ever taking it off
because she knows
he gave up the gold
and everything that went with it
to have her.

Ode to My Father On His Birthday

Every morning he wakes up at 4:30 for work, and on his days off too. He has a few cookies — the gross lemon ones that you can buy in packs of a thousand for 79 cents — and two cups of coffee (he says with the coffee, you can't even taste the cardboard cookies).

Then he packs his lunch — the same every day for the last 20 years: sardines in hot sauce, an apple or pear, and a handful of plain chips — into the purple and white pail with the pink button that I carried my lunch in through elementary school.

He puts wood in the boiler to heat our house, feeds the cat, takes the dog out, and off he goes to the factory job he hates, the factory job that put me through college, the factory job that paid all mom's hospital bills.

He is silent when he gets up and has never woke me once, his movements as gentle as his love.

Tonight I wait until I hear him snoring, then tip-toe into the kitchen. He wakes up if a pin drops so I hold my breath because I've got my mother's loud, clumsy hands.

I fill the old lunch pail with peanut butter chocolates and a small balloon that says *Have a good day*! That's code for *Try to avoid telling your boss, in great detail, how you will shove his balls up his ass.*

I put out a spread of assorted cookies, good cookies from the local bakery, with a note folded into the shape of an envelope. In gold lettering, I write *Happy 56th birthday.*

I slip back into my room and he is still snoring.

And when he comes home from work, I'll make him open presents and he will say, *You shouldn't spend money* as he unwraps the new hummingbird feeder.

Watching hummingbirds makes him happy. I love to see him happy.

Then we'll have spaghetti as he requested because he's a man of simple pleasures, and *You know, Audrey, I'm not a little kid anymore. I don't need a big dinner or a cake.*

I smile. I like this response.

He used to say, *My birthday stopped being my birthday when it became the day my wife left me.*

He didn't need to say more than that.

I felt every cruel thing she ever did, each moment, like tiny needles sewn under my skin on an endless loop.

Up, down, up, down.
Prick, heal, prick, heal,
prick.

Every day became the day my mother left me.
But we have both learned how to turn the loop off, learned to reclaim what is ours.

Today is his.

And I hope he knows that today is my favorite day.

My favorite day.

Story of My Father

I see you
in a faded red t-shirt,
strapping me into the front seat
of your beat-up truck.
I laugh and kick up my feet,
throwing fries to the pigeons.

I see you
in a blue bandana,
dragging the back of your hand
across your forehead,
sweat beading up
as you chop wood to heat our house.

I see you
slide my small hands into
orange work gloves
because I want to help you
and I feel handy picking up twigs.

I see you
rip back the pool cover,
pull me out of the water
and push oxygen into my chest.

I see you
kiss my bloody fingers
after I grab the empty olive can off the counter.

I see you
teaching me how to ice skate
and never saying a word
about how I only use one foot
because you like it best
when I do it my way.

I see you
helping me roll change
from my piggy bank

and taking me to pick out a new movie
because we never had cable.

I see you
come home from work
covered in grease and burns,
showing me the deposit slip
for my college fund.

I see you
in the living room,
gashes on your hands
held together with super glue.

I see you
wrap your tired, freckled arms
around my mother.

I see you
before her
and after her.

I see you,
young and fearless,
climbing out a wrecked car
without a scratch,
working long days at the mushroom plant
so you could party all night.

I see you
coming from nothing
and never wanting kids
because you wanted to drive your boat
down the Hudson
and not struggle forever.

I see you
before her
and after her.

I see you
asking her to stay home from work

and when she refuses,
you propose right there
on the bathroom floor.
And she says *no* the first time,
but you always told me
I just knew she was the one,
you just know when you find the one.

I see you
getting married five years later
all cleaned up in a gray suit and tie,
looking at my mother
like I've never seen anyone look at anyone,
with the man she will leave you for
smiling in the background.

I see you
working overtime
to pay her hospital bills
and making her feel beautiful
when the doctors cut off her chest.

I see you
scraping up the money
so she can go back to school
and cooking dinner
while she studies.

I see you
tangled up in her
every night
with a happiness
they only write about.

I see you
before her
and after her.

I see you
screaming,
begging her

not to leave.
I see you
waiting for her all night
with every light in the house on
knowing
she isn't coming home.

I see you
the morning after your birthday,
the morning after she finally said it:
I'm having an affair,
I love him
and I don't see you at all.

Every piece of you
held together by her love
shatters at once.

I see you
weeping

and

weeping

and

weeping.

I see you
ashamed to tell anyone
but me
that your wife left you for
a monster.

I see you
the night of my car crash,
watching me fade in and out
of sleep in the hospital,
telling me *don't worry, I'm here*
when I ask why mom isn't.

I see you
eating every burnt meal I made
like it was the best you ever had
so that I wouldn't cry
and maybe
so you wouldn't either.

Till Death Do Him Part

My father is the kind of man
who will still
answer your phone calls
and change your oil
after
you have slaughtered him.

I wish that was a metaphor.

Fortuity

There are depths
to being hollow.
Water droplets
wondering if look like you.
Am I doomed like
you.
To what do I owe
probability?
Am I subject
to what you
create?
I feel my face
shatter.
Shatter.
I see the time
condensed.
Repressed.
Is this
home?

30 Years in Four Walls

I know.

But I don't.
My response is a formality, an etiquette,
a way to fill somebody else's need for understanding,
their need for a sympathetic tongue to form the words *I know*
with sorrowful eyes and a bent mouth.
I don't know
but it comforts them anyway
the same way the same formality comforts me.
I have never really thought about it,
about the way we say things we don't actually feel
until I said, *You know, it looks different now*
and with a stiffness in his throat, my father said
No.
It will always look
the same
to me.
And this time when I say *I know,*
I really know.

I know that I can change the thick curtains,
rip up the carpets,
burn the bed,
smash the glass frames,
tear the entire room down to the studs
bare and wood and empty
then redress it like a magazine photo,
perfect, untouched like it has never been inhabited
and possesses no memory of its own
and it will still
always look exactly the same.
I know
because I've done it.

And when I look around,
it is her ironing that dress,
the one with the buttons down the front,
Audrey, does this look good on me?
It is the ruby ring she adored

and her lilac tree outside the window.
It is me lying beneath her desk as she works,
fiddling with her chair.
It is the knitted comforter across the bed
and his work clothes pressed on the end.
It is being 10 years old and coming home too early.
It is her favorite color on the bathroom walls,
and two drawers of time hidden in the closet.
It is the dark oak shelves with ornaments I made her,
A #1 Mom picture frame, a bottle of antacid,
the little book from her trip to Tennessee,
and on his side,
just one photo of me.

It is every piece of his life
and mine.
It is 30 years
in four walls
And this time when I say *I know*,
I really know.

On Making Coffee for My Father

My mother walked out
five years ago
on my father's birthday.
This year on his birthday,
the coffee maker,
just as exhausted as heartbreak,
quit.
Another sure thing
dead on the same day.

When he falls asleep,
I pull a new one out of the closet
and put it together.
I have already ripped so much of this house apart –
the coffee pot he shared with her
is just another memory on the list.
I think if I can shred the 30 years
of lost love hanging in these walls,
maybe he can heal.
But you can only erase
so much.

Two scoops of cheap coffee,
reusable filter,
enough water to make four cups
even though he'll only drink two.
Set the delay brew for 4:30 a.m.,
up like clockwork for the job he hates.

A mug that reads
You are my sunshine.
That phrase always makes me cry
because I remember
my mother singing it to me.
Like I said,
you can only erase
so much.
He will forget four nights out of five
to clean the pot
and set up the coffee for the next morning,

but I will never forget.

I will come home,
drop my bags to floor,
wipe the grinds,
tip-toe to the cabinet.
He will wake up to coffee every single morning
whether he remembers or not.

You can only erase so much
pain
but love –
love will conquer what you cannot erase.

Perspectives of a Napkin Holder

It has been three years
and I'm still not sure where I am.
I serve the same purpose
but something isn't right.
I sat atop the same aged table
for 30 years
and watched a child grow.
How they loved the child.
I watched the petty arguments
that always resolved before the
kitchen light went out.
I watched the plants perk up
on the windowsill as the sun rose,
the man sipping his morning coffee
and the woman getting up early
to join him.
And now I sit atop a new table
in a riverside apartment
where I don't belong
and I watch nothing
except sometimes
her crying.

Fight or Flight

Every time I see you
agony and fulfillment go to war inside my chest
and from my absence,
maybe you can guess which one wins.

I haven't heard from you in months.
You ask if I can do you a favor.
I want to say
I doubt it,
no.
But I say *yes.*

I park my car, whisper *give, give, give* under my breath
knowing there is never any take.
I roll my eyes and in the same moment,
drop them.
My anger collides with my sorrow,
the two things you've given me.

I do you the favor. You try to pay me.
But I don't want the money.
I could give a fuck about the money.

I say I have to leave
and throw two bags of your favorite candy
on the kitchen table.

I think back to when I brought flowers on your birthday.
I still haven't figured it out.
I felt like I was under a spell,
a drone unaware of what I was doing
until you opened your front door.

It is the same this time.

You tell me you love me. I don't believe you do.
I say it back for the second time in four years.

I say it because I can't fight anymore.

I say it because the words are meaningless
and the candy on the kitchen table is
more sincere than anything
either of us could ever say to each other.

A Dynamic at Best

I am the cracked cup
collecting grime
on the top shelf,
kept for no purpose
but perhaps sentimental value.
Kept, not out of love,
no, it is only pain disguised as love,
an obligation they said we'd have
disguised as love.

Pour your blackness into me.
Burn me until the cracks grow wider
and trick me with a touch of white
that disappears as the spoon swirls
and know I do the same to you.

Slivers

No matter how violently I thrash
I cannot make you leave.
I am a ghost to you,
still convinced if I hit harder
or yell louder
you will disappear.

You don't flinch
and I wake up with blood in my mouth.

Family Tradition

Yesterday I listened to Hank Williams Jr.
for the first time
since the last time I watched you
dancing on top of a chair in the kitchen,
furniture cleaner and dust rag in hand,
blaring his CDs.
You'd clean for hours,
singing along,
and there wasn't a sound Dad hated more
than Hank Williams Jr.
I still remember all the words,
and I still hear them in your gravelly voice.

Today I am in a record store in Boston,
just as far removed from you as ever.
I'm flipping through when impulse pulls my eyes left.
I smile, a you've-got-to-be-kidding-me smile.
It's Hank Williams Jr.,
the only record in the whole place pulled out
and lying flat on top of a genre it doesn't belong to.
I wonder why it's there.
I wonder if the universe is real.
I wonder if these things inside me that I deny
are family tradition.

The Void

I watch a woman on the plane rock her baby back and forth. She pats the child's back rhythmically, only removing her hand from him to hold herself up. We hit turbulence and her hand works faster, jolting from her baby to the wall, her baby to the wall. She slams her hand into the wall, pushes back, and her hand returns all the more gently. I watch her do this over and over, so quickly that I'm not sure the baby ever realizes her hand leaves him for the wall.

The flight attendant comes over and asks her to sit down. The woman does. But the baby begins to cry. She rises. She knows what he needs — dependence in its most innocent form. The baby doesn't make a sound just as long as she rocks him, her hand on his back. His head drapes peacefully over her shoulder. And I turn away, because I can feel my eyes welling up.

When I get home, my father says
Your mother called.
She misses you.

I can't stop thinking
about the baby on the plane.

Born and Bred

Ali was a brute,
a beagle rottweiler mix
named for Muhammad Ali.
Nobody could get near her
but she let me sit on her back
and pick up her ears,
and never so much as
flashed her teeth at me.
We shared sandwiches
and I slept in her bed,
my face buried in her stomach.

One morning Ali and I chased each other
over the small hills of snow
my father had plowed
into the corners of the backyard.
I ran,
laughing with my arms stuck out straight,
my jacket too puffy to let them fall.
Ali sprang up on her back legs,
slammed her paws into my chest
and knocked me over the bank.

I was three years old
and hanging upside down
by my feet
screaming for my mother.
I hung there crying
for a little kid's forever
before she noticed I was gone.
She pulled me up by my ankles,
my face red from
the blood rushing to it
and I ran from her.

That was the first time
I can remember
feeling scared,
feeling abandoned,

and as the years went on,
the feeling grew
and never left.

My mother was a lot like Ali.
She loved me
but she couldn't help
that she was born and bred
to be a brute.

When I Was 12

my mother got cancer
and so did Laura,
my godmother
and my mother's best friend,
my mother's only friend.
I held Laura's hand
as she screamed in agony,
her fingers falling limp between mine.
My mother never forgave herself for surviving
and that year she buried her best friend
and her father.

For my 13th birthday, she planned a trip to Florida.
She thought it'd make us happy.
She was so depressed, and so was I
even though she told me
kids don't have real problems.

The airport lost our luggage
and every night, she sat outside
chain-smoking and crying
while I laid in bed,
wanting to hold her
but I never did.

We never knew how to comfort each other
and we probably never will.

Our last night there, she got drunk
and told me
God doesn't like ugly,
and you're ugly on the inside.
She stripped naked outside the bathrooms
and changed in the open,
cursing and screaming
her hatred toward me.

The airport security guard told her
she couldn't smoke inside.

My mother called her a *bitch*
and threw her cigarette on the floor
of an art gallery.
When she wasn't looking,
I picked it up
and threw it away
even though I have never
been more afraid of anyone
than I was of her that night.

We never knew how to comfort each other
and we probably never will.

My Hero

Ten pages stapled together,
photos hardened from too much glue,
my fingers trace the creases across our faces.
I remember that purple striped shirt
and being nine years old,
stuffing fuzzy lime green hair ties in my chest
and looking up to my mother.
I smile, humiliated at the uneven lumps in the photo,
and at the little girl I still recognize
even though there is no one else to see this,
no one to be embarrassed in front of.

"My Hero" it's titled,
and it's filled with things I have forgotten
and other things I believed as a kid,
things I was too young to see through.

The first page is a phrase from my mother,
a thing she said all the time
to remind me to be good:
*It takes a lifetime to build a reputation
and one hour to ruin it.*

The last page is a photo of her with bright tan lines,
cutting her wedding cake
with my father looking at her,
smiling wide.

I've spent so much time missing that person,
missing "my hero."
I've spent so much time
thinking the mother who raised me
was a different person
than the mother who destroyed me.

But there are things I have forgotten
and other things I believed as a kid,
things that I was too young to see through.

I go back to the first page and I write,
You will never be happy
if you run back to misery
every time it cries
to remind me to be good,
to remind me to be my own hero.

Like You

I keep antacid on my nightstand
because I have heartburn,
like you.

I roll my eyes at the doctor,
piss in the cup
and eat the antibiotics
because I have bad kidneys,
like you.

I read novels for fun
and gasp at incorrect grammar
printed on commercial trucks
because I studied English,
like you.

I have your blonde hair and round face,
the chin like a wooden block
screwed onto a talking puppet's jaw,
and Dad always says,
You're just like your mother
when I flock to help old women at the grocery store
or pick up another hitchhiker.

I drink White Russians,
like you,
but I don't go too far
because I'm a nasty drunk,
like you.
And I don't want to be like you.

You always say I don't know the half of it,
that you are the one who has to live with this.

You are wrong.
I was made in your image,
and grew up sewing your scars.
There is nothing
I understand better.

But that is a poem
I am tired of trying to write.
That is a poem I do not owe you.
That is a poem about the why.
Why you are who you are
is a story that explains

but does not excuse.

You See What You Want To See

You say you're proud of me —
How can you be proud?
You don't know what I majored in,
when I graduated.
You don't know where I work.
You don't know what I'm good at,
what I'm scared of.
You don't know if I am compassionate or cruel,
if I am the one who puts the knife in
or tries with all her might to take it out.
You don't know who I hold close,
the names of my friends,
that it's over but I say *he's good* when you ask
because nothing makes my blood boil
like hearing you talk about love.
You don't know that I hear your favorite song in your voice
and there is one line I can't say out loud
without crying.
You don't know that my hair is red to mask your blonde,
that my inheritance of your physical features
makes me fear which parts of yours I have inside.
You don't know that all of the sorrow and guilt
you've asked me to carry
have long been replaced with a dull annoyance,
and somehow that feels worse.
You don't know me
but you talk about me like you built me,
like I owe it all to you.
You talk about me like I am the sole reason
for everything good and bad in your life.

I wish I could laugh at that when I am alone.

My chest used to burn when you'd forget my birthday.
This year I just hoped I wouldn't hear from you
but life is funny.
I heard from your friend too.
He sent me a card
with no name and no return address.

In all its malicious effort,
the part that hit me most was,
I've never met you,
but I feel like I know you quite well.
Informed by you and he feels like
he knows me quite well.

I wish I could laugh at that
when I am alone.

Therapy

The first woman says,
After my divorce, I had to move back in with my mother.
It was awful.

The woman next to me says,
I lost my mother to cancer, and I —
Her voice cracks
and I can feel her tears before they leave her eyes
and I would give
anything
to live with her one more time.

I put my hands on her shoulders.

Another woman says,
My mother just had brain surgery
and she's not the same.
She's distant from us.
It's really hard
trying to figure out who she is now.

My heart is racing
and the first woman says to me,
You don't have to share,
but tell us how it felt listening to others.

I feel like I am choking and I try to laugh.
I didn't share because
I am terrified of public speaking.

I start crying,
I can't tell if it because I am nervous
or because I am telling a group of people I don't know
that *I felt guilty listening*
because some people don't have their mothers anymore
and I refuse to see mine.

The woman next to me hugs me
and I whisper

How will it feel when my mother dies?

Four Months

Four months used to be the breaking point.
Four months used to be exactly how long I could stay away.
I laugh when I realize it has been one year
and four months
since I have seen you.
I stand in your doorway now
with a bag of obligation the size of my pity.
I recognize your sweater
and I wonder how many forgotten memories
are buried in my brain,
memories like that sweater,
memories that you will dig up if I come inside.
I can't come in, I have to go.
I set the bag down,
wishing I could box up my solicitude
and leave that here too.
I don't like to see you,
but I hate to see you like this.

Knots

you miss me
you miss me
you miss me
you are the one person
that I do not want to miss me

you are the one person
I have built a barricade for,
the one person
who has caused me enough pain
to stop my longing

you are the one person who
misses me
misses me
misses me

why does the knife
haunt the scar

why does birth
work this way

Just As Soon As I Get Home

There are weeks when the drive is bad. I sleep on the side of the road in a knot, with my flashers turned off because they are so fucking loud. And when I turn back onto the road with nothing but time, I think about all the people that are no longer important to me and contemplate if I wish they were. I think about how I will never become anything. I think about how it will feel when my father dies. I think about my mother and the way words fumble out of her mouth when she is drunk. I think about morbid, crazy things. Sometimes I shrug. But sometimes I cry. I cry until I can't breathe and it feels good. I feel drained in the best way. I think, *yes, you are totally insane. God, Audrey, you need a fucking therapist.* And I believe I might actually go blab to one, just as soon as I get home.

There are weeks when the drive is good. I roll all the windows down and my hair escapes out of a messy bun and spews across my face. I love that more than anything. I sing and drum my fingers on the steering wheel but the music is so loud, I can't hear myself and all I get out of it is a sore throat. I smile like an idiot because the songs remind me of things I love, lost things even. I look at the sky and all the clouds. I think about what they're made of. Yeah, water. But how do they look like that? I think about if I learned that in high school science but was too busy staring at the boy with the shark tooth necklace to remember the explanation. I think about how beautiful everything is. I think about how lucky I am. I think about pulling into my driveway. I think about how there is no other place that could ever be home. I think about what I could be and how I'm going to graduate so soon. I think about how much I love writing and how maybe people love my writing too, or one day they could. I feel complete in the best way. I think about how I should write down the good stuff. And I believe I might actually write it, just as soon as I get home.

There are weeks when the drive is good and there are weeks when the drive is bad. No matter what, every week I think about why I feel guilty that I do not miss you. I think about if it means I don't love you. Every week, I think about why I am scared to have figured out that I can live, and live exactly the same, without you. And I believe I might be able to make myself miss you, just as soon as I get home.

The Big Things Shrivel

The big things shrivel
and become the little things.
It is the little things you carry forever,
the little things that matter the most.
It is the little things that I love.

It is the little things that you left behind.

2

Pretending

The clementine burns the cuts in my mouth
but I eat it to be polite
and I pretend it's great.
I pretend, too,
that I'm not falling in love with you
twenty minutes into knowing you.
And you pretend I'm not an absolute disaster,
or do you?

I only dance when I drink vodka
and I smash your feet under mine.
You carry me, redress me like a child
and I wake up puking
and to you laughing,
You're a really bad dancer, you know that?
I pretend I don't remember almost killing you
with the "lawn mower" or the "sprinkler."

I get sick camping and shoo you away
from the dim mosquito-ridden stall.
You rub my belly in the dark
because you love me
and because you're afraid of bears.
I pretend I am not humiliated
that bits of my organs must be splattered everywhere.
I pretend you have seen
the pretty, delicate parts of me.
I pretend they exist in me
and I pretend they will keep you around.

I wonder,
was it the phone calls from my mother's driveway
or the way I sobbed during every movie
that made you discover my wreckage?
And after all of it,
you search my eyes and say,
Sometimes when I look at you
and can't believe you're real,
my heart wants to come out of its chest.

My Blazing Sun

The buildings look so small
and useless from his window
and I'm sure it is freezing outside,
biting wind and snow,
because every day since
I moved here has been.
But in this tiny bed,
with his hands folded in my hair
while he reads my favorite poems in Spanish,
I have never been warmer.

You Were So Amazed

You were so amazed
by the complete blackness of my room.
You kept putting your hands in front of your face,
trying to see them and asking me if I could tell
how many fingers you were holding up.
In the city,
there is always noise!
Always light!
Can you believe how dark it is here?

I love that about you:
the way the small things
fascinate you, small things like
me
and my sorrowful, one-floor house
in the sticks
with no light
and no noise.

You're asleep in no time,
with one arm over my leg.
I feel you jump in the middle of the night
and in a frantic, incoherent mumble
you say
What is it?!
I laugh and tell you
you're talking in your sleep.
You roll over,
with a groggy
I love you
and before I can say it back,
you're already snoring.
I rub your back as you sleep
and I hope you know
you're my favorite small thing.

Wholesome Love

You are espresso after an all-nighter.
You are the light I leave on to feel safe.
You are my coziest sweater.
You are pay day.
You are sweatpants after a day of meetings.
You are Egyptian cotton sheets.
You are a Neruda love sonnet.
You are ice cream in August.
You are wild blackberries growing in the backyard.
You are the bigger half of a wishbone.
You are a hundred tears of joy.
You are the quickened heartbeat of good news.
You are laughing too hard to breathe.
You are paint stains on the ends of my sleeves.
You are sentimental costume jewelry.
You are falling asleep to the sound of rain.
You are a full tank of gas on an open road.
You are an acceptance letter.
You are the smell of pollen.
You are a bluebird's song.
You are writing that doesn't need revision.
You are warm toes.
You are vanilla bubble baths.
You are watching the sun rise.
You are a garden in full bloom.
You are the view I hiked to see.
You are home.

My love,
you are
the best part
of all the best things.

The First Week Without You

The morning after you tell me
I am the wrong person for you,
Happiness is found in contentment
hangs from my teabag.
I crumble the paper between my fingers.
It doesn't make any sense to me.
Isn't contentment the state of being happy?
None of this makes any sense to me.

I call the resort and beg them
to refund our romantic room
with the heart-shaped pool
and mirrored bed.
They say they are sorry,
I missed the cancellation window.

Later, your grandmother calls me.
She doesn't know yet.
She says,
My heart is always with you.
I can't wait to see you!
Tears stream down my face
as I tell her I will see her soon.
I know I will never see her again.

My stomach is sick.

On the second day,
I pace my bedroom screaming
and screaming
and screaming.
I don't know how
but I manage to get dressed,
get in the car,
drive to work.
I cry at my desk all day,
humiliated.
I desperately beg you to see me
because I have not seen you in a month
and I miss you.

I miss you
so much.

On the third day,
I force myself to eat.
The café gives me the wrong order
and I take it anyway.
One of the things you hate about me,
my inability to be assertive.

Your sister asks if I want to trade poetry books.
She says, *We don't have to be strangers.*

I do not cry.

The fourth day, I meet a 98-year-old woman
who tells me she is happy
and ready to die.
She is getting her hair permed one last time
and this brings tears to my eyes.
I think, if she is happy,
I can be happy too.

I pull her stylist aside and pay for her perm
and then I drive to a state park two hours away.

It reminds me of the sculpture park
we went to last summer,
where I crashed my bike into a tree
and landed in a puddle.
I smile remembering that story,
I smile
forgetting for just one moment.

I go to a restaurant afterward
and cry in the bathroom
after seeing your favorite appetizer on the menu.
You would love the food here.
I tell myself not to call you.

I just keep telling myself not to call you.

On the fifth day, I drive hours in every direction
to see friends, to stay busy, to get you off my mind.
But somehow being around people
doesn't distract me like it should.
It only reminds me that I can't be around you.

A friend gives me a box of black and white cookies.
I stare at them, thinking of our day trips to the city.
You'd get me a black and white to try
from a different bakery each time.
I think of you on my doorstep,
all your little surprises,
all the ways you showed me you cared.

I thank my friend for the cookies
but I cannot eat them.

On the sixth day,
I count the minutes.
You are supposed to be here with me.
Today, I am supposed to see you
for the first time in a month,
wrap you in my arms
and hear all your stories from California.

I start cleaning to occupy myself
and find a beautiful letter you wrote me.
I shouldn't open it
but I want to feel your love so badly
and in these words, I do.

I just keep telling myself not to call you.

But this is where I crack.

You answer.
You have always been so calm, so logical
and I have always known that is who you are,
yet hearing the detachment in your voice
still stuns me.

You say I should throw that letter out.

Throw everything out, all the pieces of us.
I confess I can't bring myself to touch your soap in my shower,
I cannot get rid of anything.

I feel vulnerable
but at peace
with you listening.

I ask if you have been fighting the urge to ask me how my day was,
or if you are relieved you don't have to anymore.

You say,
I am not going through what you are.

Your words slice through my fragile tranquility.

I do not cry on the phone.

I can no longer show you my wounds
and know you will love me anyway.

I drive to the resort that I booked for us.
I don't know why I am here.
It is beautiful
and I sit on the staircase with my head in my hands,
and I weep
wondering why this is so much easier for you.

On the seventh day,
I wake up with my friend's face next to mine
and I can't breathe
because it's not you.
Memories of us flood me
and my hyperventilating wakes them.

We have to go.
I can't be here.

On the drive home, I try to control my breathing.
I try with everything inside of me
to relax.

In the silence,
I think about how I said I never wanted marriage or kids.
This is my fear of winding up like my parents,
my fear of failing a child.
But I never told you
that my love for you was greater than all of my fears.
I never told you
I wanted to learn Spanish to surprise you when I recited my vows.
I wanted to name our daughter Nora,
after your grandmother.

It has been a week since you told me
I am the wrong person for you.
In all my pain,
I am trying to find anger and hold onto it.
But I can't.

I can't muster anything but love for you.

What Are The Odds

I order bed sets to donate
and get a giant box of Christmas lights instead.

I am looking for a place to volunteer.
It's harder than I thought it would be.
I keep emailing churches and soup kitchens
and none of them are open on Christmas Day,
except this one synagogue in Rye.
Rye, where you live,
where I would be spending Christmas
if we didn't break up last week.

I'm supposed to make up hours at work
for the time I missed totaling my car
but my father said we could put up the tree together.
I leave work on time even though I know
it probably won't happen.

He starts screaming about how much he hates the holidays
and says I should spend Christmas somewhere else.
It's just another day,
he doesn't give a fuck.

But I do
and I thought that would be enough this year.
I thought I would be enough this year
but there is no tree
and there is no you.

I'm in bed at 7:30 and I want to call you,
ask how your day was,
ask what the fuck I should do
with all these Christmas lights.

But I already caved and called you this morning
because I had a dream about you
and woke up sweating.
I can't cave twice.

I tell myself that one day
someone will fall in love with me
and stay there,
tell myself
that one day I'll know what to do
with Christmas lights.

Always Almost

Keep in touch
is for never speaking again
and *good to see you*
is for stirring up dirt
that is almost settled.

It is always
almost settled.

Post Office

I am at the post office putting your books in an envelope. Books, and the pair of socks I borrowed from you the last time I saw you.

I had said I didn't want the last time we saw each other to be me crying and screaming. I didn't want the last time to be the breakup. So we got together for lunch. I think we both knew it would be more than lunch.

I showered. Stood in your robe and brushed my teeth. You hadn't thrown out my toothbrush yet. I got dressed, shoved my tights in my purse, and put on a pair of your socks. The familiarity of being there was painful. I didn't want the last time we saw each other to be me crying, but this was too much to hold. You looked at me with such pity.

I drove the two hours home and stared hard out over the Tappan Zee. I loved this view, this drive. I loved everything that led me to you. And even though I know I have to let go of it, I torture myself to memorize it first.

I write "hope all is well" on a piece of paper and put it in the envelope. It pains me that this feels like the only thing I can say to the person who knows every raw part of me.

We spent so much time trusting, loving, knowing. It is amazing how quickly years of devotion collapse. How quickly we become strangers.

I seal the envelope, breathe in as I write your name. The affection I found in saying your name, writing your name, all replaced now by this sinking discomfort.

I jot your address from memory. Wonder if it is possible for me to forget your zip code, your house number. Forget what color your door is. Forget how to get there.

Forget what having a home felt like.

Cold

You once told me
letting go should never be easy
like it was a rule
you were trying to convince yourself
to obey,
like *don't cheat on the test*
while you ink the answers
on the palm of your hand.

He Still Dreams About Having Sex With Me

He still dreams about having sex with me.
He tells me this in a sad voice,
as if he is relating to my pain,
as if the absence of my naked body
is torture,
as if my skin was the best thing about me.

He tells me this in a sad voice,
on my third day of not eating
and not sleeping.
I cry until I am nauseous
and I sit on the tub floor
with the water running down my back
wishing I had a mother to call
or maybe a best friend
who also thinks of me as their best friend.
That is what a mother is anyway,
right?

The Breaking

You are going to feel a pain so great
that you will swear no person
has ever felt it before,
a pain so great that you will not be able to breathe.

Your stomach will ache,
you will not sleep —
and when you do,
you will dream of your pain —
you will choke on tears
and sweat and snot
every morning
and every night
for months and months to come.
The pain will make it so you cannot see
the parts of you that exist without them.
It will obliterate everything else inside of you
so that you can only think of it.

This is the life.
This is not the last time you will hurt.

Nor is it the first.

Remember that you have felt pain greater still,
remember how time has shrunk it.
Time has made you forget what it felt like
all the times before,
crawling on your knees
for as long as it took to stand up.

You will feel this pain a hundred times over,
and a hundred times
you will crawl,
stand,
forget.

Overcoming will make you want to harden.
Don't.

There is strength in your softness.

Crawl,
stand,
forget —
what do you think makes that possible?

He Might Miss

He might miss
your tender mouth,
legs wrapped around him,
things said between sheets and half asleep.

He might miss the pressure of your thumbs
in the soles of his feet,
the work week crumbling against your palms.

He might miss phone calls during rush hour,
the enthusiasm in your voice,
how you remembered every song,
name, date, place, and thing
that was important to him.

He might miss squeezing soap down your back
and hands tracing his face,
the closeness of having someone
who knows the wall and has climbed it.

He might miss red velvet cupcakes,
two spoons in an ice cream jar,
and the way your hair looks in the morning.

He might even miss the drive.

But do not mistake this.

Know that he does not miss
you.

Vestal

I am staring down the hallway
of what used to be home,
struggling to find the gratitude
that poured out of me into this place.
I remember but cannot feel
the illumination of my chest
rising and falling
in that fourth floor window
while the wind hurled.
I remember but cannot feel
the happiest days of my life spent here,
drinking colors and light
from this brick fountain.
Now it feels only foreign,
a story made up in my mind.
My eyes fall over all the same things
and I think it's ironic how time
replaces love with revulsion.

You made this place a paradise
that is now a prison
with the gates flung open
asking me if I want to stay.

Are You

Are you listening to old hip hop
with the angry look I adore
only because I know the sweetness underneath
glued to your face?
Are you feeding yourself that bullshit
about how you do not need anyone,
about how you are strong
because you are detached?
Are you looking down your nose
at me
and everyone else who is purple
with pain?
Are you happy without me?
Are you still reading my poems,
still thinking *damn,*
the girl's amazing?
Are you still rooting for me?
Are you still thinking of me
when you listen to Frank Ocean?
Are you still playing my records,
remembering when I told you
I knew I was in love with you
the moment you played my favorite Elvis song
on your radio show
and I cried?
Are you wondering how I'm doing,
wondering if I am really gone for good?
Are you wishing I would call,
is your pride still bigger than your heart?
Are you wondering if I have heard from my mother?
Are you starting to forget
the sound of my laugh?
Are my underwear still stuffed in the corner of your drawer?
Are you wearing my favorite sweater?
Are you sleeping next to someone new,
wondering if I am too?

Never Greener

Listen to me.

The one who walks away
does not share your pain.
The one who walks away
is not concerned with you —
you,
unable to sleep,
unable to eat,
unable to dream,
unable to stand.
Your weeping is a burden,
your neediness an annoyance.
You are behind them.
They are out chasing what seems like freedom,
what seems like the sun.

But know this —
the one who walks away
surely runs back.

They gave you up in search of richer things
and with nothing to show for it,
they return with self-serving hands,
expecting you to paint their canvas white,
expecting you to morph your wounds
into love again
and again.

Listen to me.

You are freedom,
you are the sun,
and people have to live with the choices they make.

Don't you dare feel guilty.
Don't you dare think your healing is a mistake.

3

The Rules of Dating

don't watch his eyes don't laugh too loud don't research his interests
don't expect him to care about yours don't bring up your mother don't be
so honest don't compliment him don't ask too many questions don't
show weakness don't curse so fucking much don't call don't flinch when
he tries to kiss don't forget to be casual don't say anything when he
interrupts don't point out your flaws don't give him gifts don't say
goodnight don't mention your writing don't show it to him either don't
talk about what you want don't grab his hands stop stop stop stop
stop
stop thinking
stop pausing

spare nothing
scale all of you to full size

yes,
he might think you are too much, too vast, too stirred up —

but this is none of your concern

you have spent your entire life
contorting your joy
to fit in other people's mouths

stop

he will take you or he will leave you
exactly how you are

be
exactly how
you are

City Beer Hall

I want to ask him
do you make your bed every day
or do you like it messy, honest?
what song makes you cry?
what's your first memory of being let down?
have you ever looked into someone's face
and felt like your lungs were on fire?
were you braver as a child?
do you feel dead when you wake up?
how do you cut your pancakes?
what are you afraid of?
do you want to sit in my car
and listen to music
and pretend we don't want to kiss each other?

but we just met
and I have a tendency to say too much.
maybe asking too much is worse
so I don't ask anything.
I just watch him talking to the man
who happened to sit down next to him,
watch him talk to the bartender,
watch him talk to me.
I can see goodness inside him
and I hope it is real.

3 a.m.

It is our fifth date
and we haven't kissed yet
and we won't tonight because
I have vomited six times
in this beautiful restaurant.
I am laying in the booth with ice on my face,
knowing this is just my luck.
He doesn't think I should drive
and he's right,
but I feel like a burden
who should go home.

I've been with him since noon.
He answered the door in his bath robe
and I sat on the couch,
hands buried under my legs
to hide their shaking.
We went to the museum.
He pointed to a display case of stuffed birds
and told me a story about him and Drew
seeing a gigantic owl just like that one
in the middle of the road
just standing, staring.
He told me a lot about history too —
he knows a lot about history,
he's smarter than I am
and I tried not to let that show.

I get up from the booth,
apologize to the waitress again
and tip 40% for the food I couldn't eat.
He invites me back to his apartment,
says I should lay down
and even though my brain feels like
it is made of gun shots,
I am only happy.
He leads me to his bed
with the white flower sheets
and he leaves the room.
I think this is respectful and hard to find.

I tell him he can come in,
lay with me.
I keep thanking him
for letting me come back here
and he says,
what kind of person would I be if I didn't?
I consider how awful people are
and I say,
a normal person.
He starts to play his guitar
and it sounds like
I never want it to end.
I say I like Matchbox Twenty
and he plays.
I sing in my best half dead voice
and we both laugh.
We haven't even kissed yet
but I am unwrapping my baggage
in his bed sheets.
He tells me some of his secrets too.
His openness is stunning
and I don't know it yet,
but he will be the first man
whose emotions are not afraid of mine,
whose emotions can understand mine.
I don't know it yet,
but that is how I will fall
into loving a man who is leaving.

He tells me it's 11 p.m.
and I have to move my car
for alternate side parking,
but I can stay over.
I feel like I've taken up too much of his time,
I insist on going home.

I wish I had stayed.
I wish I had woken up next to him
much more frequently.

Lark

He works overnights.
It is 8 p.m.
and he needs to eat
but can't wake up.
I kiss his shoulder
and whisper *I'll be right back.*

I have always been afraid to walk down this street,
so I never have.
They call it anxiety —
I call it being a woman
in a man's world.
But it is 8 p.m.
and he needs to eat.

Three blocks.
Eyes down, key between fingers,
is this jacket big enough?
How can I make myself
smaller?
Smaller, smaller,
make myself invisible.
A man whistles from a car window
Wow! Beautiful woman!
You look like a flower.
I am walking faster,
faster.
Face to the pavement,
I don't want to be a flower.
Men in the pizzeria
cut through my humming
with *Miss, excuse me, miss, miss.*
I think maybe they are harmless
but my brain goes blank.
I grab the food
and practice running.
Tell myself not to bite my lip.
It is a nervous habit
mistaken for lure.
Two more men yell jokes to me

but I am busy running,
busy trying not to exist.

They call it anxiety —
I call it being a woman
in a man's world.

I am out of breath when I reach him,
and I lay across his stomach
heaving.

Your heart is beating fast.

I kiss his shoulder
and tell him it's time to eat.

Counting

Earlier I cried
for this empty room,
for the 10-year mess,
for the loss.
Your head is in my lap
and you ask how I feel.
I run my fingers through your hair
and down your back
and you are surprised
when I say
good.

You have put me at
total peace.
I am only thinking of suspending
this moment in time.

I am only thinking of wanting to have you for
longer.

2,838

I teach myself art
by watching you sleep.

I trace the curvature
from the bottom of your chin
to the top of your brow
and I let the words
sit idle in my mouth.

Issues With Affection

I do not know the details
I do not know if it replays in your mind
I do not know all the ways you feel

but I don't need to know any of that
to know
there is nothing wrong with you.

I don't need to know any of that
to know
any guilt or shame you carry
does not belong to you
no matter how long
it has been strapped
to the back of your throat,
no matter what happened to put it there.

You are beautiful heart,
head buried in the pillow
half smiling
anxiety perfect.
You are honest,
empathy raw
talk until my voice comes back
notice my twitching.
You are thought,
unaware of what you give
wind in my hair.
You are a snapshot of bliss,
opening your eyes
opening despite.
You are feeling,
tears sentiment
not hiding from your
shadow.
You are keys
in the same pocket
words I can't say
things I am too afraid to lose.

Anyone
would be lucky
to sleep next to you at night
knowing that.

What If

food can make you sick.
you still eat.
driving can kill you.
you still go.
friends can betray you.
you still trust.
love can hurt.
why do you stop?

pain is a possibility in every scenario, but you have forgotten
so is joy.

Be With Them

what pain taught you
to close your mouth
at the chance of a feast
when you are starving?

Let It Be The Healing

you ask about my poetry,
unaware that you are the reason
I cannot stop writing
in a time when I feared I had nothing left to say.
my body feels like it is 300 degrees
burning from the inside out
because you don't have a clue
that you have given me a gift.

I write for the barbed wire under your skin,
I write for the comfort that you cannot dream of,
for the time you think will never come,
I write for our shared wreckage.
my fingers beg to mend,
they trace these words
page after page
for both of us
because I am not good at talking,
but someone has to tell you
that you do not need to stand in one spot and bleed
any longer.

if I am to play no other part in your life,
let it be this.

Crazy

You call me crazy and think it's ok
because I call myself crazy too.
I call myself a lot of things.
I've learned to use self-deprecation
to stay one step ahead of what others might think of me.

But when I say *crazy*,
I mean hanging on words, I mean hopeful, I mean not knowing when to
give up, I mean dreaming about my fears and waking up paralyzed, I
mean bent over backward, I mean chewing on my cuticles, I mean
vomiting at 3 a.m., I mean hyperventilating on the sidewalk before
opening the door, when I say *crazy*

I mean so full of love, I mean planting gardens in graveyards, I mean
driving eight hours to help a girl I don't know, I mean spontaneous train
rides, I mean spending Christmas Day at the homeless shelter and
wishing I didn't have to go home, when I say *crazy*

I mean wanting to know you, really know you, I mean accepting, I mean
studying your interests, I mean parking four streets over in the snow, I
mean the same song on repeat for six days, I mean feeling lonely but
finding comfort in your smell on my pillows, when I say *crazy*

I mean manic talking or unable to speak, I mean no in between, I mean
the scar in the corner of my mouth, I mean vulnerability, I mean sharing
these poems, I mean putting all of myself on the line, I mean not afraid
of pain, I mean

you
are
worth
it.

When I say *crazy*,
I do not mean crazy. I mean valid feelings, I mean other people's lack of
understanding.

I have to acknowledge that you may not understand why I do this or why
I think that, and it is easier for me to laugh at myself and call myself
crazy in front of you than explain.
I have to acknowledge that you may think my openness, my honesty, my
outpour of compassion
is crazy.

And if you do,
then please,
call
me
crazy.
I will wear the word in gold, I will wear it with pride
because these are the best parts of me.

Leap of Faith

Your Instinct says that I will fix this,
I can always fix this.
I am the outlet,
the dumping ground
that twisted dandelions spring from.
Have you ever seen a weed
so fucked up and so eager to
give?

Your Instinct knows how this works:
deposit the burden into me
and withdraw your equilibrium.
It does not hesitate,
it does not have time for *please* and *thank you.*
Your Instinct runs to me
because I am a safe bet,
because I do not have the power to hurt you,
because it has never heard me say
no.

Your Instinct knows my name
but has only ever called me Leap of Faith.
I do not correct it
because it is not wrong.
It is my Leap of Faith that
invests in dead gardens
and anything else
that does not want me
but maybe will
if I breathe into it long enough.
It is my Leap of Faith
that believes your heart might be a canary
singing, in its spare time,
for my salvation.

Trying

I am cleaning his drunken vomit off the porch
and his sister asks me how I feel
about him leaving.
I tell her I am trying not to feel anything.
Trying, meaning I have envisioned
the rest of my life in four scenarios
and I don't know
if I am happy in any of them.
Trying, meaning I will never tell him
I would have waited
to move across the country with him
because despite this thick curtain of emotion,
I can still see the writing on the wall.
Trying, meaning I am always looking for
the next escape,
the next shot at temporary bliss
with every hope it will become
permanent.
Trying, meaning my best friend
is messaging me, concerned about my
"depression"
and when I say
I am just going through something,
he reminds me
that I have been going through something
for a long time.

Wind Up With

Much as I wish,
long as I stay,
I know you will not wind up with me.

But I hope
you wind up with someone
who calms you,
who accepts each part of you,
even the coping —
especially the coping,
who falls in love with you
by studying where your face has been.
I hope you wind up with someone
who helps you better yourself,
who labors for your comfort,
who pulls the past out of you
with patience and sliver by sliver,
sees it for all it is,
and cannot wait to build a future with you.
I hope you wind up with someone
who thinks of you every day
and finds new ways to show you,
who drives with the windows down
and messy hair,
who makes you feel like you are perfect.
I hope you wind up with someone
who has eyes you want to look into
during sex,
who breathes more slowly
when your arms lock around in her sleep,
who fits her elbows into the knots
of your back
and coats your sunburnt shoulders in aloe
on a great vacation.
I hope you wind up with someone
who compromises,
who always wants to hold your hand,
who laughs,
cries,

stands
with you through everything.

I hope you wind up
with someone
like me.

Something

Your fears are the same color
as my love,
two sides of the same mountain
facing different directions
and flashing red discrete.
There is something to be said
about the likeness,
about exchanging old knives
in bed sheets and on bar stools
and knowing the blades will never
carve anything new,
in knowing we won't use our hurt
against each other.
There is something to be said
about your sleeping head in my lap
and how I brace you for every pothole,
something to be said about
the magnitude of something so small,
about how trust only exists —
knowing only exists —
with a certain degree of love,
a pendulum swing of how vulnerable
we want to be
and something to be said
about lace sliding off my hips
and the delicacy of our hands
and our stories.
There is something to be said
about closeness during absence,
about playing the expression
of your face, gap in your teeth,
shape of your lips, curve of your spine,
like a video in my mind
remembering how it looked
when the sun hit your eyes
the first time you looked into mine.
There is something to be said
about how we can move each other
from 2,800 miles away,

about this thread
as thin as it could be
and somehow neither of us let it break.

It's how I know your fears
are the same color as my love,
it's how something
becomes enough.

Prism

You mistake my heart
for a broken one.
Ask me, of all the things I fear,
why not this?

I crush prisms in my jaw
and spit them into your hand,
tell you to hold my pain
up to the sun.
Watch the colors bounce off the walls —
see what I've done with it.

I am both the light and the refraction.
I have always known how to
bend,
how to turn shards
into softness.

I will make a masterpiece
out of this, out of us
and it will be

blinding.

$\underline{4}$

Art

your eyes literally glow
after you have cried,
like the stripes inside a marble
being cut in half by the sun.
I have seen so much beauty
born of your pain.
this is how I know you will be ok.
this is how I know you will always
transform the wrongs you bear into art,
into hands that never stop giving.
I wish you could see how stunning that is,
I wish I could measure it in miles
and drive you up and down that road,
pointing out your heart
in every yellow light.

Her Freeing You

Don't search for me in her.
You will not find me again.
We are each other's past
and someone else's future.

Let our history wash away
and then drain the water —
do not drown her in it.

Don't fill her with your fears.
Don't wrap her body around yours
and tell her you're not ready.
Don't make her climb the wall
for half of your devotion,
don't make her climb it at all.

Don't talk to her about me.
She will hear the admiration in your voice
even when you are criticizing me
and it will torture her.
She will wonder if she is enough,
if you will ever let go of me
and fall into her.
Don't make her wonder.

Don't make the same mistake
twice.
Don't make her pay for a pain she didn't create.

Recognize that she is good for you.
Let yourself love her.
Really love her.
Love her with gratitude.
Love her in ways you never loved me.

Leaving

my emancipation
lives under my tongue,
which is to say
I mean it
when I tell you
I am not coming back.

I Don't Want To Learn Anymore

Three weeks ago my father told me
I should get the mole on my left hand removed
before it gets any bigger.

The mole on my left hand —
I never even noticed.
Now I can't stop looking at it,
pulling my sleeve over it.

This is how timidity is born.

I think about the scar in the corner of my mouth,
the one bump turned two on my nose,
black thread sewing up the leftovers of my flaws.

Customers at work kept telling me I had something on my face.
Yeah, they're stitches,
I got the ugliness removed.
Well, most of it,
I think.

People used to make fun of the mole on my nose
and when I went to the surgeon,
he convinced me to throw in the mole on the corner of my mouth too.

He told me that he'd have to cut deep into my nose
or that mole would likely grow back.
He said it would leave a dent.
I thought that'd be even worse
so I said *no, don't go too deep.*
I will come back if it grows again.
He dragged the scalpel across the surface of my imperfections.
I blinked as a line of numb blood ran down my face.
I was 15.

I was 15
when I learned that ugly was the worst thing a woman could be.

I was 17 when I learned to add fat to that list.

19 when I learned to add opinionated.

20 when I learned to add a slut.

I was 23 when I learned that a woman can be enlightened and
brainwashed at the same time.

I was 23 when I learned that despite my condemnation of these rules and
their judges,
I subscribed to all of it.

I was 23 when I woke up sweating at 4 a.m.,
dry heaving over the toilet
because I felt worthless.
Because this world has taught me
that I am the worst things
a woman could ever be.

It doesn't matter that I can write words that move the cold,
it doesn't matter how many books I've read or how many theories I
understand.
It doesn't matter that I am creative,
that I am smart.
It doesn't matter that I never show up empty-handed.
It doesn't matter that I am honest,
that I have more compassion than my body can hold.
It doesn't matter
unless I am beautiful,
unless I am thin and quiet
and innocent.

I reject the notion, of course.
Don't we all?

Yet here we are.

Supposed To Be

The company of others is the most draining labor.
Tonight I am exhausted
from smiling,
laughing, being agreeable,
making sure I don't say too much or too little.
He barely knows me
and I am hopeful for small talk,
something mindless.
But he has all these questions
about what I believe,
what I want
and don't want.
I am agreeable
but not agreeable enough.

He tells me the purpose of life is to live for God.
I want to tell him my mother was a Sunday school teacher
and I was the altar girl,
breaking bread and reading my poetry during sermon
to all the good believers.
Look how that turned out.
I want to tell him I don't know what my purpose is,
but it is not to live for something
I don't believe in.

He tells me that marriage
is how you devote yourself to another person,
you can't have that kind of commitment without marriage.
I want to tell him you can't have that kind of agony without divorce.
I want to tell him that being legally tied to someone
has nothing to do with commitment.

He tells me that I should want to have children
because it's the way you form a bond with the person you love,
by creating another person with them,
and of course,
you must leave something behind as a legacy.
I want to tell him those are selfish reasons to have a child.
I want to tell him that we aren't all in need of a legacy,
that we aren't all so fucking important.

But I say nothing.

He tells me he's not judging me,
and he doesn't want to impose his views on me,
(Lying is a sin, doesn't he know?)
but he doesn't understand why I don't want these things,
the things he believes I should want.
I have no desire to give him an explanation
but he demands one.
I say,
to each their own
and when that isn't good enough,
I just don't think I need any of those things
to be committed or happy or whole.
He's not judging me
and he doesn't want to impose his views on me,
but he tells me
your life is directionless.

I should laugh at this conclusion.
I should tell him how absurd I think it is
for anyone to believe a white picket fence,
a piece of paper, a Bible, and a baby
can decide a person's worth.

But I watch all of my fears climb out of his mouth

and I say nothing.

Remembering the Men

Aw shit,
I think to myself as my bra splits in half.
I am waitressing
with two lopsided cups moving under my shirt
as I lift trays of chicken parm
and bite my tongue for nasty old ladies.

I don't know how this happened.
I have no boobs, I mean
I don't think I even had nipples until I was 16.
I probably don't need to wear a bra at all
but I do because I still hear that boy
in seventh grade social studies
calling me *a flat-chested cunt.*

After work
I stroll the lingerie aisle to regain my dignity.
I look up to see a man, standing and staring
as I try to find something
that isn't covered in a thousand sequins.
I hope he will turn around and walk away
and when he doesn't, I look at him
and want to scream,
Leave
me
the
fuck
alone.

I hurry as his eyes follow me
and I grab a flimsy, pink thing with gaudy jewels
that'll probably do a number on my washing machine.
I walk to the checkout,
annoyed and disgusted,
remembering that boy in seventh grade,

and remembering the man who,
with two young daughters in tow,

asked if he could have
a piece of that ass,

remembering the man
who followed me
through grocery stores aisles,
angry that I wouldn't acknowledge
his *compliments,*

remembering the man
who told me
my *man boobs*
were giving him a
half boner
the first time he saw me topless,

remembering the man
who whistled at me
as I crossed the street in July wearing shorts
and when I didn't respond, yelled,
you can't dress like that
and not like the attention,

remembering the man
who, despite being my uncle,
calls me *sexy,*

remembering the man
who tried to drag me
onto the dance floor
by my arms,
and another man
who succeeded
and smashed his
body against mine,

remembering all the times
I have felt enraged but
been too afraid to say

I do not exist for you.

Cessation

I dream of you
standing in my kitchen
with overgrown curls,
red eyes,
and a lit cigarette.
And when I turn around,
you are a shaved head
in a designer suit
telling me you wish you could kiss me but…
you point to your wedding band.

I ask if you knew you were gay
the years you spent telling me you loved me,
with all the time in between
when you made it clear you hated me.
I ask you if you treat your husband better.

You dance around the questions,
the only way you know how
to have a conversation with me.
I run my finger over the black part
of your bottom lip and down
to the beauty mark on your chest,
and I tell you
It's ok.
It's ok.

Attention Register 9

I pass his mother
in the grocery store.
She looks exactly the same,
just a little emptier
but she has lost so much
how could she possibly look
full.
I don't think she notices me
and five minutes later
the speakers in the store come on
and say *attention all shoppers,*
will Audrey
please come to register 9?
Audrey, please come to register 9.
I stand still for a minute
and decide there must be
another Audrey in the store,
a little girl in a pink jacket
crying for her mother
or a candy bar
and maybe both are at register 9.
I stare into glass pans that I know I will not buy
and enough time passes before I leave the aisle.
I glance at register 9 as I go by.
No one is there.

I remember winning her over
with letters I slid across the counter
to uninviting eyes,
letters about how I meant well,
how I wanted the best for her son,
how I was not what she thought I was
until she'd finally speak to me,
finally have me in her house willingly.
I remember the beginning,
I remember all of it.
I remember both of us crying
at the kitchen table,
I remember her apologizing,
I thought I raised him better than this.

I remember her being there at 4 a.m.
to get him off me,
remember her being there
when my own mother left.
But now I can't look into her face
and revisit those years,
not without notice,
not in a grocery store.

Attention
register 9,

please know

I was always grateful.

Time

Time creates mechanisms
to keep wounds shut,
mechanisms to keep you functioning
when you're half alive,
mechanisms to make you feel ok
about functioning
when you're half alive.

Time is the difference
between spilling your pain in the streets
and having the capacity
to focus on something, anything else
just long enough to make it
behind a closed door.

Time is the difference
between collapsing on the floor
when you are told she is dead
and kneeling at her grave
to plant tulips.

Time is the difference
between searing pain
only numbed by vodka
at the thought of your mother
not wanting you
and being able to tell the story
of her leaving
with just enough humor
to make people think you're funny
instead of unstable.

Time is the difference
between setting the alarm
four hours in advance
because that's how long it takes
to stop crying in the morning
and being able to sit across
from your heartbreak
and make small talk over coffee.

Time is the difference
between believing you will never
feel whole again
and standing on a rooftop
overlooking the buildings at night
knowing that is not the truth.

Maybe the bones of these wrongs
are never set right,
maybe the knives that carved them
never correct themselves.
Maybe they don't need to.

Maybe time is only for clotting blood
and sewing skin,
and not for erasing.
Maybe time is only the lover of gratitude
and the brother of empathy,
and not a magic wizard.

Maybe time says
these remnants float
so that you cannot bury them.
Maybe time says
you must feel this
so you can appreciate that.

Maybe time says
this
is what makes you human.

Capsulated

Coming home makes me think of you. The highway going into town where you pulled over behind me because you needed an aspirin. The diner, the first time you made me cry. Going camping, up all night even though I had to work in the morning. Spin the bottle in seventh grade, I tilted the bottle so it would land on Danielle instead of me. I was too scared to kiss you. Senior prom, your backyard, the way you looked at me. Flat tires in the rain. Trying to learn how to cook when my mother left, calling you crying, *how do I season the chicken?* French toast, you taught me and now I have forgotten. Watching movies with your family on Thanksgiving. Sending too many flowers. Bubble baths, drinking wine out of tupperware. You put your hand on my knee at the movies and I walked out. Apple picking, *can we not call this a date?* Alex's party, you too protective. Crying into your red t-shirt because he broke my heart again. Softball sized hickeys, walking up and down back roads. Swimming at the waterfall. Senior skip day, the sculptures. Ambrosia, *she doesn't know how cute she looks right now.* Paintball in your clothes. Your mother finds condoms in your sock drawer, I laugh. Sleep on your sister's floor and wake up to roosters. The first time we ever hung out, Ramshorn, pink flip flops on ice. AP English, she called on you and I passed you the answer. *If I were single, I'd kiss you right now.* Dress-up day. Middle school science class, you're the boy with the shark tooth necklace. The scar on your forehead, shape of your mouth, way your hair curls, sound of your laugh. Bottles at the creek behind your house. Mud fights at the lighthouse, spelling your name in the sand. Lobster earrings from Maine. Your cheesecake. Watching you work on your boat. AZUL, I look for that car every time I pull in. Cooking in your kitchen, the wrench on your faucet. Drinking hard lemonade on the porch, Siamese cats coming up the steps. The pink perfume that gave you chills. *Point to the door if you're just attracted to me, point to the closet if you're in love with me.* You point to the closet. Sushi in Kingston, the bakery in Round Top. Haven't been there since you. Running errands, spending four hours trying to pick out a new pair of glasses. Bringing you lunch at work when you did construction, *you look nice.* I was wearing that gray shirt that twists in the front. I think of that day every time I put it on. The Saloon, orange juice, dream catchers, caves. *Leave nothing but footprints.* Getting you a job, we stop speaking but you still help me carry trays. You hear I'm moving. *She makes me happy, but not as happy as you could've.* I cry. *Can I kiss you? No.* You do anyway, I'm glad you do. Just kissing, all night, six hours. I've never felt anything like that — I mean that, I really mean that. Calling out of work, making my bed, listening to Kendrick Lamar. I hear the song again a year later and I have to pull over. Helping me pack my bags. The night I move, you sit next to me in the booth at dinner. I email you *I love you.* You know I like to write it down. *I always wondered if you were as sexy without clothes as you are with.* Her ring on your dresser. You love me, you don't love me. The cruise, the wind, the tears when you said you care about me. The man in the train station trying to win his daughter back. The tie I stole, it looked good on you. Your head on my shoulder, asleep. Your half smile, your ears pressed into mine. You on top of me. *Can we just be friends?* I ask you to leave. *I'll date someone who says the right thing sometimes and you'll date someone who makes your head turn. But it's never going to be me and you.* Snooping around the neighbor's abandoned house. My dad catches you there, *my parents are looking for a place.* I think that's a lie. Maybe that's how you miss me. I have to believe you miss me sometimes.

Letter to the Next

I want to get out of the shower with mascara under my eyes and red blotchy cheeks and have you standing there looking at me like I am a figment of your imagination, like you have seen the seven wonders of the world in your hands.

I want you to appreciate my bleeding heart, how I cope with pain, the manic way I write. I want you to appreciate the little green dress, the inflection in my voice when I'm telling a funny story, the eyes that never wander.

I want to lie in bed with you in the middle of winter eating ice cream and laughing. I want to spend the whole day tasting your cheeks, hearing stories about your childhood, about your joy, about your fears. I want to see your flaws, I want to dip them in honey.

I want you to remember to ask how my day was. Remember when something important is happening, remember to ask *how'd it go?* Remember names and stories. Remember that I don't like picking seats in a movie theatre. Remember to put on Lee Brice or Train when I am panicking. Remember to compromise.

I want to show up on your doorstep with your favorite dessert. I want to wake up early to eat breakfast with you. I want to blindfold you in the car and not tell you what adventure I've planned for the weekend. I want to explore your interests and share mine with you. I want to admire the freckles on your back and massage the knots in your neck. I want to spend time with your friends. I want to leave lipstick-stained postcards on your windshield. I want my love to be a constant surprise.

I want to dive into you.
I want to build something bright and fresh and honest.

But I don't want you
if you are too afraid,
too selfish
to dive with me.

Prayer to a God I Don't Believe In

I am drinking coffee in the sun,
staring through exhaustion at the pavement
when a voice from behind me says,
excuse me.

I turn and see a woman
with her hand out, pointer finger missing
and a long scar up her hand to her wrist.
I'm not asking for money.
Please just
hear me.

Her eyes are teary.
I look into them,
remember the times I have felt
desperation and sorrow
and multiply them tenfold.

I just had surgery
and all the shelters are full.
Please, can you get me some food?
I am so hungry.

I study the deep wrinkles of her face,
frozen for a moment
as if I don't know what my answer will be.
I always know what my answer will be.

Yes, of course.
What do you want to eat?

Anything.

Well, what kind of food do you like?

She points at the burrito place behind us,
Could I just go in there?

I walk inside with her

and she keeps thanking me.
She says she has been asking people for food
for two hours.

I ask, *are you from around here?*

No. Mississippi.

Do you have any family here?

No, and the shelters are full.

So where do you stay?

I am staying in a tent
in the woods.

She orders her food
and I say, *get a drink too,*
you have to stay hydrated.

Before we part, she says,
I am 70 years old
and I have Stage 4 cancer.
I am trying to get a sleeping bag.
Pray for me.
Please pray for me.

I nod my head,
I will.

And maybe I will,
maybe I will say a prayer to a god I don't believe in,
a prayer for how we came to this,
a prayer for humanity,
a prayer for every hungry stomach,
a prayer for every skull of hatred,
a prayer for a sleeping bag
large enough
to warm the world.

For Bobby

It is early September
when the doctor says you have a week to live.
You tell my father and he fixes your car windows
because he doesn't want you to freeze this winter.

When you die five days later,
my father doesn't know.
He shows up at the hospital
and looks at your empty bed.
It is Friday
and he asks the nurses what room they've moved you to.
They stare at him blankly.
He asks three more times
before one nurse says,
I'm sorry.

The last time he saw you was Tuesday.
You couldn't talk
but when he put his ear to your mouth,
you somehow managed to whisper
I love you.

You died Thursday,
with my father's cross around your neck.

Your brother Johnny says the wake is Saturday.
He looks just like you.

I go because even though he won't say it,
I think my father needs me there.
I go, too, because I loved you
for being my father's greatest friend.

His throat wells up on the front steps of the funeral parlor.
He says,
Bobby just turned 56 on July 5, you know that?
His hands are shaking.
He tries to sign the guestbook
but only manages "G" before he drops the pen.

Sign my name.
He pulls a bandana out of his suit pocket
and holds it to his eyes.

They bury you in his cross necklace
and he keeps saying he wishes he gave you something nicer.
If I knew he was going to die,
My God, if I knew.

At the cemetery, old buddies of yours and Dad's tell me,
Take care of your father.
He's getting older.

I weep over your casket
because I can't take away my father's pain,
because I can hear you yelling
Gaaaaaary! down the driveway,
because there are so many stories I still want you to tell.

I weep
because my father will die one day too.

For Bobby, Part 2

I get chills driving into the graveyard.
You are buried across the street from Dad's parents
and I garden there often
but I haven't been here since your funeral.
You don't have a headstone yet
but you are easy to spot
because how could I forget
watching my father stand here like a statue
one sledgehammer away from crumbling,
and because the grass still hasn't grown back.
I see footprints in the dirt
that your body is under
and I rake them smooth.
Can you hear me singing?

I am thinking of a story Dad likes to tell
about you two getting into trouble
when you were kids.
My father running fast as hell down the street,
you chasing behind him,
smoking pan in your hands.
He laughs twice as hard
every time he tells it.

I sit behind your plot
digging my hands into the ground
and planting flowers.
So many flowers.
Blue and white and yellow and pink and purple.
What else can I do?

I just keep saying,
Dad misses you so much, Bobby.
God, he misses you
like you wouldn't believe.
I keep telling you
you're going to look really good
because you told Dad when you got sick
that you didn't want to be buried

like a dog.

So many flowers.
Blue and white and yellow and pink and purple.
What else can I do?

I twist my fingers around old roots,
ripping the long vines out of the dirt.
I dig and dig until the outsides of my hands ache.
I pat down the dark mulch,
make sure every plant is surrounded,
make sure it's perfect.

When I get home,
Dad wants to see a photo of the flowers.
He stares,
takes off his glasses,
and pull his eyes down.

He misses you so much, Bobby.
God, he misses you
like you wouldn't believe.

What else can I do?

You Must Keep Laughing

look at you
stressed and settling
and making up rules.
you cry all week
and spend Sunday laughing in the mirror.
laughing at the way
you commit to others
but never yourself.
laughing at the way these cruel people
bring you to life.
laughing at how it's ever been a question
why you feel empty.

laugh, you must keep laughing.
I know you will not change,
you don't want to.
your weakness is pure and kind
and it is the only thing
you are proud of.
so laugh, laugh to keep yourself sane,
laugh at how the givers of this world
endure the greatest suffering.

my darling,
your heart is the boldest thing about you
and the scariest too.

How Finishing Feels

Is it somehow shocking to know
a rock that has been through the ocean
is still just a rock?
It spends years in turbulence
hopeful to come out somewhere brighter
doing something better
just to wind up
amongst five hundred others
on the dirt it ran from.

Elegy

There are people who will search
the rest of their lives
to find your love,
spend the rest of their lives
wishing for a friend like you,
a lover like you,
a heart ripped wide open like you,
and they will never find it.
They will grieve
without knowing why,
feel empty without knowing why,
without knowing you,
without knowing
that you took your own life
because you never felt
whole,
because patience is a virtue
you were not born with,
because you were too much good
in a bad place.

And every time I taste cheesecake
or hear wind chimes
or see the sun peering over a mountain
or watch a father comfort his daughter,
I will weep
knowing that these were the things
you didn't want to miss,
the joys you stuck around for
until one day
they were not enough.

Train From D.C.

My father has been telling me
not to smile at strangers
since I was old enough to understand
but it never quite clicked
so here I am sitting on the train
going face to face,
smiling at everybody.
Next thing I know
this little old man is sitting next to me.
He's talking to me the whole ride
and the language barrier is a little rocky
but I manage.
He's asking why I'm not married,
I'm laughing.
He says, *you pretty girl, everyone like you*
and I have 100 things to say to that
but I just smile,
ask if he's married.
He says, *yes, 32 years*
and I say, *I bet she's more than pretty,*
I bet she's your whole world.
He gives me his restaurant business card,
tells me to come the next day.
He wants me to try his food
and meet his son, his unmarried son.
Tell his wife that "Uncle Tom" sent me.

The woman in front of me is running
her hands through her hair
and I can see boulders on her back.
I know what the combination of frantic
and exhausted looks like,
I wear it too.
She is black and she is beautiful
and she is typing to someone.
She writes, *I'm ok.*
Just ok?
I mean given the current circumstances in America right now...
She closes the message,
checks her American University email.

She is black and she is beautiful
and I really want her to be more than ok.
I want this heap of Earth to feel more like a warm bed
and less like a brand new graveyard
that's never really been new.

The man across from me takes off his shoes.
He closes his eyes and moves his toes around.
He is old and tired and should be retired,
should not have sore feet.
Uncle Tom is still smiling,
a bag of laminated menus in his lap
and 50 holes in his shirt.
He says he lived in Argentina once,
had a Chinese restaurant there
before opening one here.
He says he loves to cook,
he doesn't ever want to stop cooking.
Then he asks, *do you like tramp?*
I apologize, try to guess what he means.
Finally he says, *president.*
Oh, Trump.
The woman in front of me exits the train.
I say, *no.*
I do not like anyone who promotes
racism and sexism.
He says something I can't make out,
something to do with Korea and China and Taiwan.
His voice shakes.

My glance falls to the man wiggling his toes.
I almost get off at the wrong stop
and he opens his eyes,
reads my confusion,
tells me in an accent I can't place that
Shady Grove is next.
I thank him.
He looks at me in a way I can't describe,
fixed on me like I am made of magic.
And I wish I was.
I wish I could scoop the woman,

Uncle Tom, and this shoeless man
into my arms,
bundle them all up
and pull the pain out of them
like a burned rope.

Cycles

You moved all the time but this is the only house I can remember.
We thought the whole world was in that giant field,
and we liked to play "survivor,"
seeing if we could stay outside all day
eating blackberries off the bushes,
climbing trees, and swimming in the creek.
We'd stay out there for as long as we could because
going inside is when the survival really started for you.

You crossed the dirty kitchen tiles
and poured canned spaghetti into a bowl for us.
I opened the drawer to get a spoon,
my hand landing on a vial of white-yellow rocks
and a short pipe.
We were so young
but we both knew.
You slammed the drawer shut.
I never mentioned it
and neither did you.

We went our separate ways as we got older
but adored each other all the same.
You got pregnant when we were sixteen.
I smiled at you across the lockers.
I thought, *this will save her*.

You showed up at my house in your beat-up car
with a little black dress
for me to wear to our graduation.
You were struggling,
but I'd never seen you happier
than when your daughter's finger wrapped around yours.
I'm going to give her everything, you said
and I believed you.

Five years later
I see you parked outside the grocery store.
I lean into your window.
Breathing in your smoke,

I tell you, *it's so good to see you,*
wow, you've gotten so thin.
I hug you,
feeling your bones.
I do a lot of coke, you say laughing.
In my mind, I see you slam the drawer shut one more time
and the tears well up behind my eyes.
I was doing heroin because it's cheap,
but I didn't really like it.
Your voice is easy, like everything is ok,
only tense when you tell me,
I would never put drugs before my daughter
like my mother did.
You fill with the hatred you've carried inside you
since the days of canned spaghetti and neglect,
then slowly lull back to easy,
like everything is ok.
I resent her,
but I am thankful for what she put me through
because it made me who I am today.
I want to ask you if you have ever considered
who you might've been
if you weren't who you are now.

I want to ask you
if you will slam the drawer shut again
when your daughter opens it.

For Joe

Has it been four years
or five since we last spoke?
Between your tendency
to guzzle vodka
and my tendency
to blur years together,
I guess we'll never figure it out.

You always said turtles reminded you of me.
I still don't know why
but it's still bittersweet
to hear you say it again.

Memories

The bad memories sometimes feel foreign.
Distant, like they are someone else's stories
playing in my head.
Stories I heard too many times,
too long ago.
But the good memories,
I always know those are my own.
They always feel like
me.

To Know Her

I never paint my nails.
I don't want flakes of polish chipping into my mouth
while I tear up my cuticles.
I never file them either.
When I was a kid,
my mother filed her nails constantly —
in the morning with her coffee,
while she read murder stories online,
during Samuel L. Jackson movies —
but she always hid the file when she was done
because she knew I was afraid of it.
I cannot deny that she was sometimes a good mother.
I also cannot deny that even Satan fell from heaven.

My front teeth are not even,
though I don't think anyone notices that
or the beauty mark on the left side of my face.
The dimple in the corner of my mouth is from a scalpel,
and the mark they cut off my nose when I was 15
is growing back.
I bite my lips
and wear lipstick to cover the skin I take off.
I always need to have something in my hand:
a straw wrapper,
a receipt,
a finger from my other hand —
something to pick apart.
Perpetual nerves are my bag.

I am not aggressive.
I am a doormat in fact,
except
when it comes to my body.
I am the one who gets to chew through this flesh,
nobody else.
I have kicked men to the curb
for trying to guilt me into sex
or acting as if their pleasure is above mine.
I don't have the patience for their entitlement.

I once threw an uppercut into a man's jaw
because he called me a whore.
I slapped another across the face
for grabbing my ass again
after I told him not to.
I was almost certain he was going to hit me back.
I was ready to fight,
I wanted to fight.
Nothing has ever made me lose my shit
quite like a man who thinks his dick should be my priority.

More so than nail files,
I am terrified of first kisses
and getting blood drawn.
Both have always started with me screaming.
The phlebotomist usually takes it better
than the man whose tongue I almost sever.
All of my fears are equally stupid.

Therapy is parking in an overgrown field and staying
until I find peace or until I lose my voice,
whichever comes first.
Love has been similar.

A few years back, my only coping skill
was drinking enough vodka in the bathtub
to go from sobbing to laughing in 10 minutes.
I used to watch myself in the mirror.
It was like a movie,
a movie I couldn't stand up in,
a movie that ended horribly.
I had nothing left in my arsenal after that,
but I do now.

I've been told not to derive happiness from something else,
to find it only within myself.
Please — as if the two do not go together.
The distinction comes only in figuring out which to rely on.

I find happiness
in the mother playing peek-a-boo with her child in the supermarket line,
in the person holding the door for an elderly man,

in the owner who lets the dog explore without yanking him away,
in seeing the sunset over the Tappan Zee,
in having dinner with my father,
in the man playing a beautiful song on the street,
in the stranger smiling back at me,
in Christmas decorations from my childhood,
in waking up next to someone who loves me,
in coffee with an old friend.

But I do not rely on these things.

I rely on the parts of me that glow
when I am alone
like sunlight slicing through the dark.
I rely on these torn up hands
that climb out of my mouth
to cure neurosis with the grip of a pen.
I don't know what poetry is
and maybe I'm doing it wrong,
but I am happiest
when I am writing.

Speaking

what a curse —
the gift of words,
the crippling fear of
enunciation.

I Will Say *Not For Your Convenience*

When the man in the elevator
puts his hand low on my back,
then lower,
pulls me in
and whispers
you are very pretty,
I will remember
being voted most outspoken
twice in high school,
I will feel that rage unlock,
I will say
fuck you
but
he will only hear
thank you
because today I am voted
23 and terrified.

When the man leaves me,
says my love is like a blind spot,
real and invisible at the same time,
and it's just too much effort
to turn his neck,
I will say *I do not come twice*
but he will only hear
please.

When the man tells me
I would look better
if I knew how to do my hair,
if I fixed my makeup better,
I will pour liquid foundation in his eyes.
I will say
how do I look now?
but
he will only hear
probably.

When the man holds my hand,

says he does not know
how he feels about me,
I will say
I am not going to wait
but
he will only hear
32 love letters,
one for each day he is gone
and one for his birthday.

When the man nods toward me
and says *ass* to his friends,
I will remove seven layers of clothing
and strangle him in the street.
I will say
I am a person
but
he will only hear

silence.

94302257R00074

Made in the USA
Columbia, SC
25 April 2018